MIDLOTHIAN PUBLIC LIBRARY

3 1614 00184 2526

W9-ANP-630

-DISCOVERING THE NEW WORLD-

-A Chronology of-

NORTH AMERICAN
EXPLORATION

by Sarah Powers Webb

Consultant:
Richard Bell
Associate Professor of History
University of Maryland, College Park

CAPSTONE PRESS
a capstone imprint

Connect Books are published by Capstone Press,
1710 Roe Crest Drive, North Mankato, Minnesota 56003
www.mycapstone.com

Copyright © 2017 by Capstone Press, a Capstone imprint. All rights reserved.
No part of this publication may be reproduced in whole or in part, or stored
in a retrieval system, or transmitted in any form or by any means, electronic,
mechanical, photocopying, recording, or otherwise, without written permission of
the publisher.

Library of Congress Cataloging-in-Publication Data
Names: Webb, Sarah Powers, 1967–author.
Title: A chronology of North American exploration / by Sarah Powers Webb.
Description: North Mankato, Minnesota : Capstone Press, 2017. | Series:
Connect. Discovering the new world | Includes bibliographical references and index. |
Audience: Age 8-14. | Audience: Grade 4 to 6.
Identifiers: LCCN 2016010282|
ISBN 9781515718673 (library binding) |
ISBN 9781515718703 (paperback) |
ISBN 9781515718734 (eBook PDF)
Subjects: LCSH: North America—Discovery and exploration—Chronology—Juvenile
literature. | Explorers—North
America—History—Juvenile literature.
Classification: LCC E101 .W413 2017 | DDC 970.01—dc23
LC record available at http://lccn.loc.gov/2016010282

Editorial Credits
Brenda Haugen and Alesha Halvorson, editors; Ted Williams, designer;
Kelly Garvin, media researcher; Laura Manthe, production specialist

Photo Credits
Alamy/National Geographic Image Collection, 33; Getty Images/Bettmann, 31;
Newscom: akg-images, 7, 27, 45, Album/Prisma, 15, Glasshouse Images, 9, Peiro
Oliosi/Polaris, cover, World History Archive, 5, 11, 34, 41; North Wind Picture
Archives, 13, 17, 21, 23, 25, 29, 30, 39; Superstock: Acme Imagry/ACME Imagry,
18-19, George H.H. Huey/age footstock, 37

Artistic Elements: Shutterstock: Adam Gryko, Caesart, ilolab, Joanna Dorota,
Picsfive

Printed and bound in Canada.
009648F16

CHAPTER ONE

The "First" Explorer (1492–1504)

On August 3, 1492, Christopher Columbus left Spain in search of Asia with 90 sailors and three ships: the *Nina*, the *Pinta*, and the *Santa Maria*. Asia traded many important spices, foods, gems, and cloths that the Spanish wanted. Traveling the land route to Asia by foot was dangerous and long. Sailing to Asia meant a ship had to travel around the southern tip of Africa. Columbus thought he could reach Asia faster if he sailed west. King Ferdinand and Queen Isabella of Spain approved his **expedition**.

expedition—a long trip made for a specific purpose, such as for exploration

caravel—a small, light sailing ship

Columbus bid farewell to the queen of Spain before departing for the New World in 1492.

THE AGE OF EXPLORATION: 1450–1700

The Age of Exploration lasted roughly between 1450 and 1700. The invention of the **caravel** allowed European explorers to travel farther across the ocean than before. During this time, the Spanish, French, English, and Dutch competed against one another to claim new territories around the world. New territories meant quicker trading routes, more military forts, land, and riches.

Explorers sometimes sailed under other nations' flags. Expeditions often required a lot of monetary support. Sometimes explorers couldn't find that support in their own country. Adventurers supported by European countries explored and named major waterways in North America. They also explored, named, and settled regions and cities we know today.

DISCOVERY: 1492

Columbus was a master **navigator**. He studied the tides, the winds, and the clouds to track his ships' locations across the Atlantic Ocean. But weeks turned into months and his crew became restless. Some wanted to return to Spain.

Two months later, on October 12, Columbus's crew finally spotted land with white beaches and dense green forests. He named this island San Salvador, which means "Holy Savior" in Spanish. Today's historians don't know exactly which island Columbus first discovered, but it is believed to be in the Bahamas. Friendly people greeted Columbus's crew. Columbus called them Indians because he thought he had found the East Indies, islands off the coast of Asia. Columbus claimed the land belonged to Spain. He said the people on these lands were Spanish subjects.

But Columbus was surprised. He thought he was close to Asia. The people he found were the Taino (TYE-no) Indians, not Asians. The Spaniards had hoped to trade goods, but the Taino traded nothing that the Spanish valued. Columbus noticed that some Taino had gold rings in their noses. Through sign language he tried to discover where there might be more gold.

A.D. 1000
Vikings settle L' Anse aux Meadows, Newfoundland.

AUGUST 3, 1492
First Voyage of Christopher Columbus; he left Spain with three ships: the *Nina*, *Pinta*, and *Santa Maria*.

OCTOBER 12, 1492
Columbus discovers the Bahamas.

Christopher Columbus

VIKINGS IN AMERICA: A.D. 1000

Christopher Columbus was not the first European explorer to reach what became known as the **New World**. Viking explorers settled in a place they called Vinland on the tip of Newfoundland, Canada, around A.D. 1000. Vikings came from Scandinavia, now known as the countries of Norway, Sweden, and Denmark. Today this Canadian settlement is known as L'Anse aux Meadows.

> **navigator**—a person who can plan and control the course of a ship's position
>
> **New World**—the name for what is now North and South America in the 1500s

7

LA NAVIDAD: 1492–1493

Columbus continued to explore the Bahamas, as well as the islands now known as Cuba and Hispaniola. He found new plants, such as sweet potatoes, papaya, mango, and pineapple, which were previously unknown to Europeans. While he explored Cuba he captured native peoples, including the Taino—both men and women—to take back as slaves to Spain.

As Columbus's crew sailed around Hispaniola, the *Santa Maria* ran aground and sank. From the wreckage, Columbus built a fort that he called La Navidad. He left 39 seamen to manage the fort while he reached Spain. By March 15, 1493, Columbus returned to Spain. He never found much gold, but he **exaggerated** the riches he discovered. Columbus wanted to meet King Ferdinand and Queen Isabella's expectations. He also hoped to return and create a settlement to gain more riches.

> **exaggerate**—to make something seem bigger or more important than it really is

Columbus kidnapped
American Indians and
brought them back to Spain.

**OCTOBER 13-23,
1492**

Columbus explores
the Bahamas.

**OCTOBER 28-
DECEMBER 5, 1492**

Columbus explores Cuba.

**DECEMBER 6-26,
1492**

Columbus explores
Hispaniola.

DECEMBER 26, 1492

The *Santa Maria* runs
aground off the coast
of Hispaniola.

**DECEMBER 26, 1492-
JANUARY 16, 1493**

Columbus continues to
explore Hispaniola and
builds La Navidad.

**JANUARY 16-
MARCH 15, 1493**

Columbus returns
to Spain.

SECOND VOYAGE: 1493–1496

Because Columbus claimed the islands he discovered were a part of Asia, his voyage was considered a huge success. It took him only seven months to return to Spain, and no lives were lost, which was highly unusual. He returned to Spain a hero. The king and queen awarded Columbus the title "Admiral of the Ocean Sea." By May 1493 Columbus was planning his second voyage. The goal of his second trip was to gain lands and riches for Spain. The royals gave him permission to **colonize** Hispaniola.

On September 25, 1493, Columbus left Spain a second time. This time he took 17 ships. More than 1,000 men traveled as his crew. One of the men in his crew was Juan Ponce de Leon. De Leon was a young but experienced soldier from Spain.

> **colonize**—to start a settlement in a new place

MAY 28, 1493
King Ferdinand and Queen Isabella award Columbus the title of "Admiral of the Ocean Sea".

SEPTEMBER 25, 1493
Columbus begins second voyage.

Columbus' ships sailed toward Hispaniola. He was anxious to check on the men he'd left in La Navidad. Finally, on November 28, they came within site of the fort. All that remained was a burned-down ruin. Every man in the fort had been killed. The Taino told Columbus that while he was away, the 39 Spanish men fought amongst themselves. Some had left the fort and enslaved three to four Taino women each. The Taino men had grown angry at the use of their women as slaves. They had burned down the fort and killed all the Spaniards. The exact truth is lost to history.

Columbus presented the king and queen with American Indians and treasures from the New World in 1493.

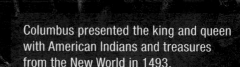

NOVEMBER 3-27, 1493
Columbus sails around islands including Dominica, Guadeloupe, the Virgin Islands, and Puerto Rico.

NOVEMBER 28, 1493
Columbus sails to La Navidad and discovers the fort has burned down and the crew is dead.

HISPANIOLA: 1494–1496

Columbus was upset about losing the men and his fort. But his first goal was to search for gold and riches for Spain. In January 1494 he founded a new fort on Hispaniola called La Isabella.

Columbus became known as a **brutal** and unfair leader. He and his soldiers, such as Ponce de Leon, forced the Taino to search for gold or face severe punishment or even death. The Taino found small amounts of gold but never the quantities that Columbus wanted. They became so exhausted and depressed that 50,000 of them killed themselves at one time to avoid slavery.

Rumors of Columbus's behavior reached Spain. Queen Isabella was against Columbus enslaving the Taino. On April 20, 1496, Columbus decided he had to return to Spain to defend his actions to the king and queen. Before he left, he had his brother, Bartholomew, establish a new city called Santo Domingo.

> **brutal**—extremely cruel or violent

Europeans continued to search for gold on the island of Hispaniola.

JANUARY 6, 1494
Columbus founds
La Isabella.

APRIL–SEPTEMBER 1494
Columbus explores
Hispaniola and what are
now Cuba and Jamaica.

1494–1496
Columbus mines for gold
on Hispaniola; Taino
natives are forced into
mining and slavery
against Queen Isabella's
wishes; 50,000 Taino
commit suicide at the
same time over forced
labor conditions.

APRIL 1496
Bartholomew
Columbus establishes
Santo Domingo.

APRIL 20, 1496
Columbus returns
to Spain.

THIRD VOYAGE: 1497–1500

By April 20, 1497, Columbus had convinced King Ferdinand and Queen Isabella to grant him permission for a third voyage. But the royals had doubts about his leadership. They only approved him taking about 350 people, less than half the number of people he took on the second voyage. Yet Columbus had trouble finding enough people to go. Many had heard of the Indian attacks and Columbus's brutality. But the king and queen gave criminals a pardon if they agreed to sail with Columbus. He and his crew finally set sail on May 30, 1498. This time, instead of experienced sailors, Columbus took criminals and inexperienced seamen.

COLUMBUS'S LAST VOYAGE: 1502–1504

Columbus restored some of his trust with the royals with a sincere apology. He claimed his loyalty to the crown and explained that his mistakes had been caused by the love of exploration. He received permission from King Ferdinand and Queen Isabella to make a fourth voyage, but not to Hispaniola. In 1502 Columbus sailed to the New World searching for China. During the 1502 trip, Columbus's ships broke down due to disrepair and age. He was stranded on the island of Jamaica for nearly a year. Finally, in 1504, Columbus returned to Spain. He never understood that he had found a new continent and had been nowhere near Asia.

APRIL 20, 1497	MAY 30, 1498	AUGUST 31, 1498	AUGUST 23, 1500	OCTOBER 1500
Columbus receives permission from King Ferdinand and Queen Isabella for a third voyage.	The third voyage begins.	Columbus arrives in Santo Domingo, Hispaniola.	Francisco de Bobadilla arrives from Spain to investigate Columbus.	Columbus returns to Spain in chains aboard the ship *La Gorda.*

During Columbus's third voyage, trouble brewed in Hispaniola. A top officer, Francisco Roldan, encouraged a **rebellion** against Columbus. Some of the men felt Columbus's leadership in Hispaniola was too brutal. In one case, Columbus ordered 100 lashes for a worker because he failed to fill Columbus's pantry with enough food. Complaints against Columbus reached the king and queen in Spain. In August 1500 the royals sent an official, Francisco de Bobadilla, to look into the situation and take over Hispaniola. It was clear from the beginning that Bobadilla intended to arrest Columbus—and he did.

In early October 1500 Columbus returned to Spain in chains. Upon meeting with the king and queen, Columbus explained himself and claimed his loyalty to their service. But they forbade him to ever return to Hispaniola.

rebellion—a struggle against the people in charge

In 1498 Columbus and his crew set sail in search of mainland Asia.

SEPTEMBER 1501
Columbus receives a partial pardon from King Ferdinand and Queen Isabella, but the royals forbid him from returning to Hispaniola.

MAY 9, 1502
Columbus begins fourth voyage.

JULY 1502– JANUARY 1503
Columbus explores what is now Panama and Costa Rica searching for a water or land passage to Asia.

JUNE 23, 1503– JUNE 28, 1504
Columbus becomes stranded in Jamaica due to ailing ships.

NOVEMBER 7, 1504
Columbus returns to Spain.

CHAPTER TWO

Early Exploration (1505–1542)

Juan Ponce de Leon had decided to stay in Hispaniola and establish a **plantation**. In 1505 he established a town called Salvaleon (*sahl-vah-lay-OAN*). Here de Leon became a successful farmer and rancher. The main crops he grew were sugar cane and corn, called *maize*.

But de Leon still craved adventure. He thought he might know where he could find more fortune—on an island the Taino called Borinquen, or the Spanish name, San Juan Bautista. Today Borinquen is called Puerto Rico. Some historians think de Leon may have led a secret expedition to San Juan Bautista hunting for gold in 1506. But certainly by 1508, de Leon led an official expedition to San Juan Bautista. He only found small amounts of gold, but King Ferdinand respected de Leon enough to make him governor and let him build gold mines on the island. De Leon forced the Taino to mine for gold and start a sugar cane plantation.

1505
De Leon establishes a town called Salvaleon and starts a successful plantation.

JUNE 1506
De Leon likely explores Borinquen, called San Juan Bautista by the Spanish, for the first time.

AUGUST 12, 1508
De Leon conducts first official exploration and colonization of San Juan Bautista.

AUGUST 14, 1509
King Ferdinand appoints de Leon governor of San Juan Bautista.

Between his plantation on Hispaniola and his mines in San Juan Bautista, de Leon became a rich man. He also became known as an effective governor. But his leadership was not without trouble. By 1511 the enslaved Taino rebelled. There was much fighting, but eventually the Spanish subdued them. The Taino were no match against the Spanish horses and firearms. Also, Christopher Columbus's son, Diego, claimed San Juan Bautista rightfully belonged to him as a descendant of the explorer. Diego fought for control over San Juan Bautista and won. By spring of 1511 de Leon still held favor with King Ferdinand, but he no longer served as governor of San Juan Bautista.

plantation—a large farm where crops such as cotton and sugar cane are grown; before 1865, plantations were run by slave labor

Juan Ponce de Leon

SPRING 1511
De Leon puts down a Taino rebellion.

MAY 5, 1511
De Leon loses control of San Juan Bautista to Diego Columbus and is no longer governor.

BIMINI: 1512–1513

King Ferdinand suggested de Leon set out on another expedition to search for possible new settlement sites. The king wanted to reward de Leon for his loyal service and for his loss of Puerto Rico. In February 1512 the king gave de Leon a contract to explore, settle, and govern Bimini, an unexplored island area to the north.

By March 1513 de Leon took three ships and headed into unexplored waters. On March 27, 1513, the explorers spotted what is now known as the Florida peninsula. De Leon called the land he first saw that Easter Sunday *Pascua de Florida*, Spanish for "Easter of Flowers."

FEBRUARY 23, 1512
De Leon receives a contract from King Ferdinand to explore, settle, and govern the unexplored area of Bimini.

MARCH 4, 1513
De Leon and his crew set sail on first voyage to the islands of Bimini.

MARCH 27, 1513
While searching for Bimini, de Leon discovers Florida.

APRIL 2, 1513
De Leon and his crew land near present-day Jupiter, Florida.

De Leon sailed farther north with his crew and first came ashore April 2, 1513. No one knows for sure exactly where de Leon and his crew landed, but today it is believed to be near Jupiter, Florida. On April 20 they had a hostile encounter with native warriors, likely from the Ais (*AH-es*) tribe. Neither side suffered serious injuries. De Leon sailed farther up and down the coast, around the southern tip of Florida, and into what is today Tampa Bay, in the Gulf of Mexico. In June 1513 hostile Calusa (*kah-LOOS-ah*) warriors met the Spanish ships with darts and arrows. About 80 of the warriors attacked the ships. De Leon responded with cannons to scare the Calusa away. Because of the hostilities, de Leon was not able to explore very far inland during the trip.

De Leon and his crew explored the Jupiter, Florida, area for about three weeks.

APRIL 20, 1513
De Leon's crew encounters hostile warriors, likely the Ais tribe.

JUNE 1513
De Leon sails to present-day Tampa Bay, Florida, and encounters Calusa warriors.

OCTOBER 19, 1513
De Leon's ships return to San Juan Bautista.

FLORIDA: 1513–1521

In October 1513 de Leon's ships returned to San Juan Bautista. By April 1514 he left for Spain to share his discoveries with the king. He had returned to San Juan Bautista by 1515. But in January 1516, King Ferdinand died. De Leon returned to Spain in 1516 to secure his titles and privileges with the new king, Charles I, Ferdinand's grandson.

It was not until 1521 that de Leon was able to return to Florida. He intended to start a permanent colony. In February 1521 he set sail to Florida's west coast to find a good settlement location. He and his crew found what they thought was a deserted beach and started unloading their supplies. Today it is believed that he landed near Fort Myers, Florida. The crew explored the area for several months. During this time Calusa warriors attacked de Leon's crew. During one battle in early July 1521, de Leon was hit with an arrow in his upper leg. His men rowed him out to his ship for safety, but de Leon's wound did not heal. The arrow may have been poisoned. De Leon's ship sailed to nearby Havana, Cuba. By the time the ship arrived in Cuba, de Leon's health was failing. Infection had spread in his wound, and he died before the end of July 1521.

APRIL 1514
De Leon returns to Spain to share his new discovery with King Ferdinand.

1515
De Leon returns to San Juan Bautista.

JANUARY 23, 1516
King Ferdinand dies.

NOV 1516–MAY 1518
De Leon returns to Spain to secure his position and titles with Ferdinand's grandson King Charles I.

Several battles took place between de Leon's crew and Calusa warriors.

FEBRUARY 20, 1521
De Leon sets sail once again for Florida, landing near present-day Fort Myers, Florida.

FEBRUARY–JULY 1521
De Leon and his crew explore and try to colonize areas near present-day Fort Myers, Florida.

EARLY JULY 1521
De Leon is wounded in a battle with Calusa warriors.

LATE JULY 1521
De Leon dies of his wounds in Havana, Cuba.

JACQUES CARTIER: 1534

The Spanish weren't the only explorers in the New World. King Francis I of France wanted his country more involved in the exploration of the New World. He hoped a Frenchman would discover the **Northwest Passage**. One Frenchman, Jacques Cartier (*DZAWK kahr-tee-AY*), had excellent navigation skills. On April 20, 1534, he led a crew of two ships and about 60 men across the Atlantic Ocean to the coast of what is now Newfoundland. French seamen knew the waters around this coast for their abundance of fish. Cartier sailed along the coast of Newfoundland. He did not find a water passage to China, but he explored the Gulf of St. Lawrence. Cartier claimed the coastal lands he saw for the king of France.

> **Northwest Passage**—a supposed water route across the northern part of North America to get from Europe to Asia more quickly

Jacques Cartier

CANADA: 1534

Throughout his travels, Cartier saw the native peoples who lived there. They were likely Huron (HYOO-ruhn) Indians. The Huron came to the coast to fish and catch seals. The French studied the Huron. For two days the groups eyed each other. Then, Donnacona, the Huron chief, signaled for the visitors to come ashore. Cartier learned that the Huron called their village Kanata, so the entire region became known as Canada.

The Huron told Cartier stories of a place called Saguenay (*SAY-goo-en-ay*) in the forests of the west. They told the French that gold and precious jewels could be found there. Cartier wanted to explore it, but he had to return to France by the end of the summer to avoid the fall storm season. He insisted on taking Donnacona's two sons with him.

In France, Donnacona's sons, Domagaya and Taignoagy, learned French, so conversation became easier. They told Cartier about a big river, a river so long no one had seen its end. Cartier believed this river might be the Northwest Passage to China. The king agreed to fund another trip for Cartier.

APRIL 20, 1534
Cartier sets sail from France looking for a water passage to China.

JULY 1534
Cartier explores the coast of Newfoundland and the Gulf of St. Lawrence and meets Huron chief Donnacona.

LATE SUMMER/ EARLY FALL 1534
Cartier returns to France and takes Donnacona's two sons with him.

Cartier was greeted by Chief Donnacona and other Huron Indians.

MONTREAL: 1535

On May 19, 1535, Cartier set out for Canada again. This time he had three ships, about 100 men, and his two Huron interpreters. The young interpreters directed Cartier to the great river that emptied into the Gulf of St. Lawrence. Later this river would become known as the St. Lawrence River. On September 7, the ships sailed to a Huron village called Stadacona. Cartier was determined to find Saguenay. He wanted to go past Stadacona, so he took a ship and about 50 men and traveled upriver.

As Cartier sailed upriver, the river grew shallower, and his crew had to continue in smaller boats. On October 2 they reached a large island. Hundreds of Hochelagans (*HOASH-uh-LAH-ganz*) greeted them and invited them to a large village called Hochelaga. Hills rose above the village of Hochelaga, which Cartier named Mont Réal, meaning "Royal Mountain." The city is now called Montreal.

Cold weather had arrived, so Cartier decided he and his crew should stay in Canada instead of risking an ocean voyage in winter weather. He returned to Stadacona and moved his supplies into a fort his crew had built.

scurvy—a disease caused by a lack of vitamin C that causes extreme weakness and bleeding gums

MAY 19, 1535
Cartier sails for Canada on second voyage.

SEPTEMBER 7, 1535
Cartier reaches Stadacona.

OCTOBER 2, 1535
Cartier reaches the village of Hochelaga and names it Montreal.

WINTER 1535-1536
Cartier and his crew spend a harsh winter in Canada; many men come down with scurvy.

Cartier and his men were unprepared for Canada's harsh winter. Without help, it was difficult for the French settlers to obtain much food. Some in his crew came down with **scurvy**. The Hurons taught them how to cure scurvy by drinking a tea made from tree bark.

Spring came and Cartier once again captured the chief's sons, the chief, and several others. He returned to France. He wanted them to tell the king directly about the mysterious place of Saguenay. But Cartier's captives died in France due to exposure to new diseases. Because of wars in Europe, it was several years before the king of France sent Cartier back to Canada to start a colony. Between 1541 and 1542 Cartier led a third exploration to form colonies in Canada. It was unsuccessful. He returned to France once again in October 1542.

St. Lawrence River

MAY 6, 1536– JULY 15, 1536
Cartier and his crew return to France.

MAY 13, 1541
Cartier sails on a third voyage to Canada to start a colony.

OCTOBER 1542
Cartier is unsuccessful in establishing a colony and returns to France.

CHAPTER THREE

Conquistadors (1538–1542)

In April 1538 an experienced explorer from Spain, **conquistador** Hernando de Soto, set sail for the New World. King Charles I of Spain had recently named him governor of the colony of Cuba. De Soto landed in Cuba the following month and began preparations for exploring Florida. He had heard stories about prosperous settlements and rich resources. He used his wealth to create a new expedition.

By mid-May de Soto and nine ships sailed for Florida, likely landing near modern-day Tampa Bay. He wanted to explore the region known as "La Florida," which included not just the modern state of Florida, but a good portion of what is now the southeastern United States.

> **conquistador**—a Spanish explorer who came to the Americas in the 1500s and claimed large areas of land for Spain; *conquistador* means "conqueror" in Spanish

APRIL 1538
De Soto sails to Cuba.

MAY 18, 1539
De Soto sails for Florida.

JULY 15–OCTOBER 1539
De Soto marches through Florida, capturing and killing native peoples, such as the Calusa, Timucuan, and Apalachee.

WINTER 1539–1540
De Soto and his explorers camp near present-day Tallahassee, Florida.

De Soto's expedition marched throughout central Florida. Along the way, they encountered and battled local tribes, such as the Calusa, Timucuan, and Apalachee peoples. De Soto captured many people from these tribes to serve as slaves and translators. Those who didn't cooperate were whipped or sometimes burned alive.

By October 1539 the Spanish were close to modern-day Tallahassee, Florida, where they spent the winter. Ships anchored in ports nearby to resupply the army. There the men heard rumors of a spectacular kingdom to the north called Cofitachequi (*co-FIT-a-cheh-kee*). It was supposed to have gold, silver, and precious pearls.

De Soto gathered 600 men and about 220 horses, large dogs, and hogs. The men would eat the hogs while underway.

CORONADO: 1540

De Soto wasn't the only conquistador from Spain exploring the New World. Francisco Vasquez de Coronado set out from Mexico in February 1540. He led a separate expedition to search for the mythical Seven Cities of Cíbola (*SEE-bow-lah*). It was rumored that Cíbola held treasures of gold.

Coronado took 300 men and more than 1,000 Aztec allies and slaves on his expedition. The Spanish also brought many sheep and pigs along for food. From Mexico, they crossed into barren land that is now the state of Arizona.

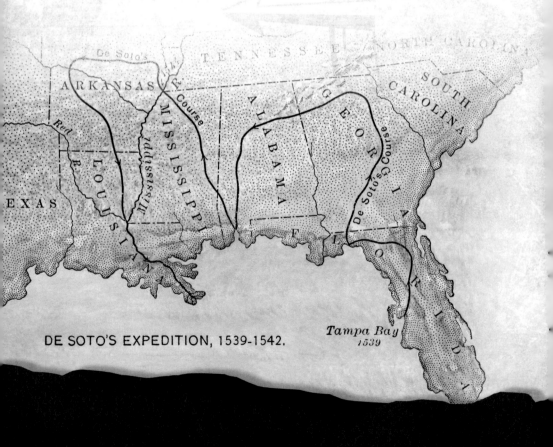

DE SOTO'S EXPEDITION, 1539-1542.

Tampa Bay
1539

Coronado was on a mission to find gold and riches in the Southwest.

COFITACHEQUI AND HAWIKUH: 1540

In the spring of 1540, de Soto's expedition traveled through present-day Georgia and South Carolina. In early May, exhausted and half-starved, they found the village of Cofitachequi. It is thought that this village was located near present-day Camden, South Carolina. The chief was a woman, known as the Lady of Cofitachequi. She showed the Spanish great kindness. But de Soto didn't find the gold and gems he expected. The Cofitachequi tribe had pearls, but the Spanish thought they were ruined. The Cofitachequi removed pearls from freshwater oysters using fire, which turned the pearls black. That didn't stop the conquistadors from taking the pearls.

American Indian city of Hawikuh

FEBRUARY 1540

Coronado marches north from Mexico City in search of the mythical Seven Cities of Cíbola.

SPRING 1540

De Soto marches through Georgia and South Carolina.

MAY 1540

De Soto finds the village of Cofitachequi, near present-day Camden, South Carolina.

In July 1540 Coronado and his expedition marched through hot deserts, finally reaching Hawikuh, the first of the Seven Cities of Cíbola. Instead of finding a wealthy city, they found Zuni (ZOO-nee) Indians living in mud and stone houses. Coronado tried to claim the village and its lands for the Spanish king, Charles I. The Zuni did not want to be Spanish subjects. A battle began, and the Zuni warriors aimed for Coronado, the leader. Coronado was easy to spot in his shiny armor. He was knocked unconscious by stones, but two of his men pulled him to safety. The Spanish finally overpowered the Zuni and took over the town. Coronado then discovered that the Seven Cities of Cíbola were really just poor towns nearby.

BATTLE OF MABILA: 1540

By the fall of 1540, de Soto's party came upon King Tascalusa of the Atahachi village near present-day Montgomery, Alabama. Tascalusa was a very powerful chief. When de Soto made his usual demands for food and slaves, at first Tascalusa refused. De Soto put him under guard. Angered over being captured, Tascalusa agreed to give de Soto several men to carry baggage. He said all the food would be supplied to the explorers in the village of Mabila, thought to be near present-day Selma, Alabama. But Tascalusa had played a trick on de Soto. The chief's warriors prepared a surprise attack on the Spanish at Mabila.

Many American Indians perished in the Mabila battle.

On the morning of October 18, 1540, de Soto, Tascalusa, and about 40 Spanish men entered the village of Mabila. Several hundred warriors had hidden themselves inside the houses. They burst forth and attacked de Soto and his small party. De Soto and a few of his men managed to escape the gates of the village.

De Soto organized an attack around the walls of the town. After several attempts, the Spanish broke through the walls and set fire to the town. In the end, hundreds of Choctaw Indians died, and the town was destroyed. Nearly half of de Soto's troops were wounded in battle—about 250 men—and 13 to 35 died. The Spanish lost most of their supplies in the fire, which included the pearls from Cofitachequi.

-DISCOVERY FACT-

In the late summer and fall of 1540, Coronado searched in other directions for gold and valuable jewels. He sent small scouting parties to explore different areas of what is now the southwest United States. One party discovered the Grand Canyon. They were the first European explorers to see it.

QUIVIRA: 1541

During the spring of 1541 Coronado was headquartered at Tiguex (*TEE-gway*), between modern-day Albuquerque and Santa Fe, New Mexico. He had heard of a rich land called Quivira (*KEE-vih-ruh*). Coronado trusted stories of a Plains Indian captive at Cicuye (*SEE-ku-ye*), called "The Turk." He told Coronado that Quivira had gold and silver.

On April 23, 1541, The Turk led Coronado's expedition to Quivira. Coronado did not know Quivira lay to the north, in present-day Kansas. The Turk misdirected the expedition into Texas. When Coronado confronted him, The Turk said that Quivira was a plot by the Pueblo Indians at Tiguex to trick the Spanish. He said the Pueblo hoped that the Spanish army would fail and die. How the Pueblo truly felt is lost to history. Coronado put The Turk in chains, and then turned north in late May. The expedition arrived at Quivira in July. Coronado saw that the village was nothing more than another poor town with grass huts. Coronado sentenced The Turk to death.

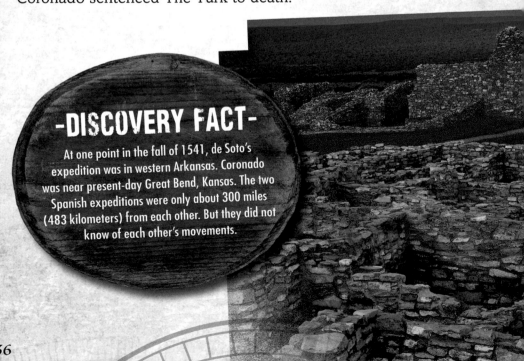

-DISCOVERY FACT-

At one point in the fall of 1541, de Soto's expedition was in western Arkansas. Coronado was near present-day Great Bend, Kansas. The two Spanish expeditions were only about 300 miles (483 kilometers) from each other. But they did not know of each other's movements.

The Spanish conquistadors never found a golden empire to **plunder** and conquer. Coronado's expedition returned from Quivira to Mexico City in April 1542. By mid-May de Soto showed signs of serious illness, possibly malaria. De Soto died of his illness near Guachoya (*gwa-CHO-ya*) along the Mississippi River on May 21, 1542. To hide his body from the nearby hostile warriors, his soldiers buried him in a log that sank to the bottom of the Mississippi River.

> **plunder**—to steal things by force, often during a battle

Quivira

SPRING 1541
Coronado's expedition makes headquarters in Tiguex, between modern-day Albuquerque and Sante Fe, New Mexico; Coronado hears stories of golden riches at Quivira.

APRIL 23, 1541
Coronado leads an expedition to Quivira.

JULY 1541
Coronado arrives in Quivira and discovers it is a poor town with grass huts.

FALL 1541
De Soto's expedition travels to western Arkansas, while Coronado's expedition is located in near present-day Great Bend, Kansas.

APRIL 1542
Coronado's expedition returns from Quivira to Tiguex, then to Mexico City.

MAY 21, 1542
De Soto dies along the banks of the Mississippi River.

CHAPTER FOUR

French and English Exploration (1600–1700)

The French continued their quest for new lands and resources. In 1603 an experienced seaman from France, Samuel de Champlain (*shom-PLAYN*), joined an expedition to the St. Lawrence River in Canada. On May 26, 1603, the explorers arrived at a French trading post called Tadoussac. There, they set up trade with the local Innu people.

Champlain explored the St. Lawrence River all the way to present-day Montreal. He covered the same territory Cartier had traveled nearly 60 years earlier. He returned to France on September 20, 1603.

On April 7, 1607, Champlain set sail on a second voyage. King Henry IV wanted Champlain's crew to establish a permanent colony. In June 1604 the explorers started a settlement on an island called Sainte-Croix (*sahn-KWA*), meaning "Holy Cross," which is in modern-day Maine.

MARCH 15, 1603
Champlain sets sail with an expedition from France to explore Canada.

MAY 26, 1603
Champlain arrives at a French trading post called Tadoussac and sets up trade with the local Innu people.

SEPTEMBER 20, 1603
Champlain returns to France.

APRIL 7, 1604
Champlain sets sail on a second voyage to develop a French settlement.

The winter of 1604–1605 proved harsh, and many settlers died from scurvy. They all decided they needed a better site for a colony. Over several trips during 1605, Champlain and the colonists explored the coasts of Maine and Massachusetts. Champlain traded with many tribes along the way, including the Micmac, Souriquois, and Wampanoag peoples. The explorers discovered many excellent settlement sites. But they decided to build their new settlement at Port Royal in modern day Nova Scotia. During the winter of 1605–1606, the settlers again suffered from the effects of scurvy. By May 1607 the colony had failed, and the settlers returned to France.

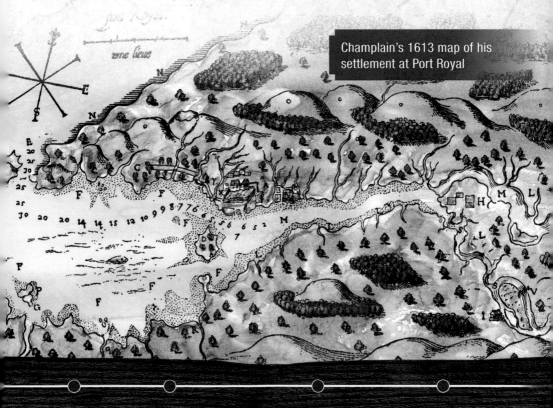

Champlain's 1613 map of his settlement at Port Royal

MAY 19, 1604
Champlain explores the New England coast looking for a colony site.

JUNE 1604
The explorers started a settlement called Sainte-Croix, in modern-day Maine, but the colonists suffer through a harsh winter and decide to look for a new colony site.

1605–1607
Champlain explores the northeastern coasts of modern-day Maine and Massachusetts and starts a new colony called Port Royal in Nova Scotia.

MAY 1607
Port Royal fails, and the settlers return to France.

JAMESTOWN AND QUEBEC: 1606–1609

The English also wanted to explore the New World. On December 6, 1606, King James I approved a plan for the Virginia Company to set sail for the new continent. In early 1607, 104 English men and boys arrived in North America. By May 1607 they founded the colony of Jamestown in modern-day Virginia. This colony became the first permanent English settlement in North America. Captain John Smith helped establish the colony. In 1609 John Smith was injured at Jamestown in a gunpowder accident and returned to England to recover.

Meanwhile in 1608 Champlain tried to convince the French king, Henry IV, that the Port Royal settlement failed because it was built on the wrong spot. He wanted to return with colonists to build a new site along the St. Lawrence River. The Algonquin (*al-GONG-kin*) Indians called the area "Quebec." The king approved Champlain's plan.

By May 1608 a new French expedition had arrived and started building the Quebec settlement. But it was not an easy time. That winter was unusually brutal. Scurvy spread when food supplies ran low, and several settlers died.

DECEMBER 1606
The Virginia Company sets sail for modern-day Virginia.

MAY 1607
The Virginia Company colonists settle Jamestown.

1608–1609
Champlain starts building a settlement at Quebec.

1609
John Smith is injured in Jamestown and returns to England.

Samuel de Champlain

ROYALTY OVERSEEING EXPLORATIONS

Ruler	Country	Reign
King Ferdinand II of Aragon and Queen Isabella I of Castile	Spain*	1475–1516
		1474–1504
King Charles I	Spain	1516–56
King Francis I	France	1515–47
King Henry IV	France	1589–1610
King James I	England	1603–25
King Louis XIV	France	1643–1715

* Ferdinand and Isabella were married in 1469, but they ruled the regions of Aragon and Castile separately in the country now known as Spain. Spain was not a nation-state until 1516.

EXPLORATIONS: 1609–1632

Between 1609 and 1616, Champlain traveled back and forth between Canada and France. He kept up good relations with the Huron during this time. He tried to establish a successful colony in Canada—known as New France—throughout these years.

Meanwhile, another experienced English explorer, Henry Hudson, was in the Netherlands seeking support for a new voyage from the Dutch East India Company. He planned an expedition to find the Northwest Passage. In March 1609 Hudson's expedition traveled up the river that now bears his name, the Hudson River.

THE MISSISSIPPI RIVER: 1682

Another French explorer, Robert Cavelier de La Salle, had an idea to sail to the mouth of the "Big River," now known as the Mississippi River. He wanted to start a colony of his own. King Louis XIV of France approved La Salle's plan. By February 1682 La Salle had gathered enough supplies and money to travel down the river. By April 9 his expedition sailed into the Gulf of Mexico. La Salle went ashore near present-day Venice, Louisiana, and claimed the river and all the lands whose waters fed into it for France. He named this vast area *Louisiana* in honor of King Louis XIV.

1609–1616	MARCH 1609	APRIL 17, 1610	JUNE 21, 1611
Champlain seeks support for Quebec and builds a relationship with the Huron Indians.	First voyage of Henry Hudson. In searching for a Northwest Passage he explores the present-day Hudson River, New York.	Second voyage of Henry Hudson begins. He explores present-day Hudson Bay and becomes stranded in ice during the winter.	After the ice melts, Hudson's crew stages a mutiny. Hudson is never heard from again.

On a second voyage in April 1610, Hudson's ship arrived at what is now Hudson Bay. By late October the ship became stranded in ice. On the morning of June 22, 1611, after the ice finally broke, some angry crewmembers staged a **mutiny**. Hudson, his son John, and a few other faithful crewmembers were set adrift with few supplies. Henry Hudson was never heard from again.

In 1614 Smith returned to the New World on a whaling ship. He is responsible for naming the region of New England, and areas within it, such as Massachusetts and Plymouth. He thought the area would be good for settlement. Later Smith talked with the Pilgrims and offered to be their advisor in a new settlement, but they turned him down. These Pilgrims arrived in Massachusetts in 1620, starting an English colony at Plymouth.

By July 1629 an English fleet forced Champlain to surrender Quebec. They took him back to England as a prisoner. Champlain knew England and France had been at war, but he didn't know that the war over Quebec had already ended. The English released Champlain in November 1629. As part of the peace treaty between England and France, Canada and Quebec returned to French ownership in 1632. Champlain had become known as the "Father of New France."

mutiny—a rebellion against someone in authority

JUNE 1614
John Smith explores the New England coast.

NOVEMBER 1620
English Pilgrims begin the Plymouth colony in Massachusetts.

JULY 29, 1629
The English force Champlain to surrender Quebec and take him back to England as prisoner.

NOVEMBER 1629
The English release Champlain.

APRIL 9, 1682
La Salle reaches the Gulf of Mexico and claims the land for King Louis XIV; La Salle names the area Louisiana.

CHAPTER FIVE

A New World (1700)

During the Age of Exploration, many European kingdoms raced against one another to establish colonies and plunder the wealth and natural resources found in the New World. Some explorers, such as Cartier and Champlain, set up good trade relations with American Indian tribes such as the Huron. Some explorers, such as Columbus and Coronado, enslaved and brutalized American Indian tribes, including the Taino and Pueblo. Over time, American Indian tribes lost their traditional hunting grounds and ways of life as Europeans began colonizing the New World.

Plants, animals, and diseases moved between Europe and the New World. Europeans brought rice, coffee, bananas, and wheat to the Americas. They also introduced horses and pigs to the New World. Some historians estimate that as many as nine out of 10 of the American Indians in the New World may have lost their lives to diseases brought by the Europeans.

Explorers returned to Europe with items, such as tobacco, tomatoes, beans, pumpkins, corn, potatoes, and chocolate. Because of these daring European explorers, the world became linked in a global exchange like never before. Not all exploration ended by 1700. But settlements along the coasts and waterways of North America created a new network of trade. These trade routes began a new period of colonization.

Diseases that Europeans brought, such as smallpox and the measles, severely reduced American Indian populations.

Glossary

brutal (BROO-tuhl)—extremely cruel or violent

caravel (KAIR-uh-vehl)—a small, light sailing ship

colonize (KAH-luh-nize)—to start a settlement in a new place

conquistador (kahn-KEE-sta-dohr)—a Spanish explorer who came to the Americas in the 1500s and claimed large areas of land for Spain; conquistador means "conqueror" in Spanish

exaggerate (ig-ZAJ-uh-rate)—to make something seem bigger or more important than it really is

expedition (EK-spuh-dish-uhn)—a long trip made for a specific purpose, such as for exploration

mutiny (MYOO-tuh-nee)—a rebellion against someone in authority

navigator (NAV-i-gay-ter)—a person who can plan and control the course of a ship's position

New World (NOO WURLD)—the name for what is now North and South America in the 1500s

Northwest Passage (NORTH-west PAS-ij)—a supposed water route across the northern part of North America to get from Europe to Asia more quickly

plantation (plan-TAY-shuhn)—a large farm where crops such as cotton and sugarcane are grown; before 1865, plantations were run by slave labor

plunder (PLUHN-dur)—to steal things by force, often during a battle

rebellion (ri-BEL-yuhn)—a struggle against the people in charge

scurvy (SKUR-vee)—a disease caused by a lack of vitamin C that causes extreme weakness and bleeding gums

Read More

Bial, Raymond. *The People and Culture of the Huron.* First Peoples of North America. New York: Cavendish Square Publishing, 2016.

Gunderson, Jessica. *Christopher Columbus: New World Explorer or Fortune Hunter?* Perspectives on History. North Mankato, Minn.: Capstone Press, 2014.

Petersen, Christine. *Learning about North America.* Do You Know the Continents? Minneapolis: Lerner Publications, 2015.

Critical Thinking Using the Common Core

1. Why was Columbus forbidden to travel to Hispaniola in his fourth voyage? (Key Ideas and Details)

2. How did the Spanish explorations in the south and west compare to the French explorations in the north? (Key Ideas and Details)

3. What were some of the results of the Age of Exploration? (Integration of Knowledge and ideas)

Internet Sites

FactHound offers a safe, fun way to find Internet sites related to this book. All of the sites on FactHound have been researched by our staff.

Here's all you do:
Visit *www.facthound.com*
Type in this code: 9781515718673

Index

JUV
970.004
MIC